ESSENTIALS FOR REVIT FAMILIES 2016

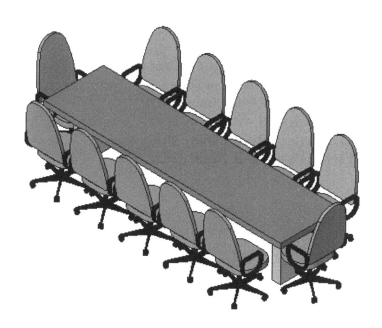

Published by: BearCat Publishing © Aug 2016

The terms "Revit" and "Autodesk" are registered trademarks of Autodesk Inc. I would like to thank Autodesk for creating such innovative and great products that are revolutionizing the building industry.

ISBN-13:
978-1517055400
ISBN-10:
1517055407

Other published work includes:

Creating Revit Family Content (2009)
Revit Family Creation 2010
Essentials of Revit Family 2011
Essentials of Revit Family 2012
Essentials of Revit Family 2013
Essentials of Revit Family 2014

Building Revit Families

A key skill required to make Revit your ally is learning to build families. These come in every shape and definition.

Mastering this skill will make you useful and marketable as there are many Revit Operators however few understand how to create families.

This is a skill which is only learned through application of knowledge and practice.

Very few Revit Classes and books provide in-depth information on this subject. This is because most instructors and authors do not have the street cred to cover the subject.

I started publishing this book in 2009 and with the intervening Revit releases I have kept the book updated.

Revit has grown and improved over the years to become the lean trim software which we appreciate today.

A vital part of learning Revit is not the pushing of buttons as much as it is understanding the concepts.

I have been fortunate to be the CAD/BIM Manager at three corporations and have led the march moving from AutoCAD to Revit.

Why Build Content?

Now that you have had experience using Families in the Project environment, you have discovered as with many CAD Products the "out of the box" version leaves something to be desired in terms of unique content. There is a lot of potential content not supplied with the generic program which you might need created to display your design intent.

To fully achieve your Design and even more important the desired look and feel of your Project Model, custom Family objects are needed to enhance the presentation and functions of your creations.

It is sometimes important to your presentations and scheduling to show the actual interpretations of the actual item instead of the rough generic version which is available in the out of the box version of Revit.

Classes of Families

There are 5 classes of families in Revit Architecture:

System families
Loadable families
Hosted Families
Annotation families

In-place families

All elements in Revit (substitute the word family) are system families or loadable families.

Loadable families (those that you create or find in the Revit Family Library) may also be combined to create nested and shared families.

Non-standard or custom elements, which are Project specific and will never be used in any other project, are created using in-place families which are only in the Project where they were created.

System Families

You can think of Revit as if it is a molecule with each atom of it a Family (Element) in one form or another.

The Revit software consists of assemblies of Families. Whether the Family is a View such as a Floor Plan or Roof Plan, Schedule, or ashtray it is nothing but a relational collection of information used in the database which is the Project Model.

Even Views are nothing more than a structured Family with its own standard parameters!

System families are the basic building blocks of Revit. System families are walls, roofs, ceilings, floors, and other elements which you would use to define the structure of your Model.

Anything which is part of the building structure is usually a System Family. Other common System Families which affect the project environment built into Revit are items such as Levels, and Grids. Yes, even

Grids and Levels are specialized versions of families hard wired in the Revit platform.

System families have been predefined inside the Revit program. These cannot be loaded into your projects from external files, nor may you save them in locations external to the project. System Families come predefined in the "out of the box" Revit software. They may be duplicated and modified however only inside the project model you are using.

If you wish to make your own custom version of a System Family you may. This is done by creating a "Duplicate" of the existing Family, renaming it and editing any of its parameters, such as materials or size to become a unique Family located within your Project Model.

They cannot be saved outside of the Model.

Go to the Element Type properties of the Family.

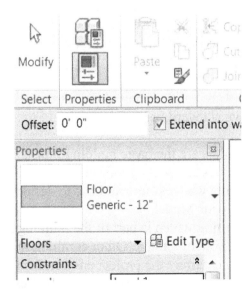

Select "Edit Type".

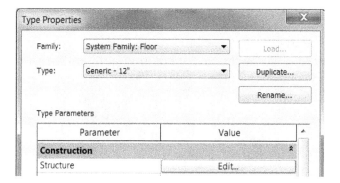

In the Type Properties dialog box select "Duplicate". Give the new Family a unique name, and then you may begin making modifications to it while maintaining the integrity of the original System Family which we used as the base for building the new Family.

Loadable Families

An loadable family is used to create building components. These include annotation families such as tags and symbols. These are saved as an external .rfa file. The suffix of a loadable Family has an .rfa extension and if you click on this file in Windows Explorer it will open the family in the Revit Family Editor.

Loadable families create the building elements which would usually be installed as separate physical items of the building structure, such as windows, doors, lights and furniture.
Because of their highly customizable nature, loadable families are the families which you will commonly create and modify in Revit Architecture.
Unlike system families, loadable families are created as external .rfa files, saved to your company's family library or imported and loaded in your projects.
        Loadable families may containing different types (size variations or materials) and are created using type catalogs, which allow you to load multiple variations of the same basic Family (such as multiple window sizes of the same design).

Annotation Families

The annotation family is a 2 dimensional family used to create annotative text objects or symbols. These families usually contain text such as Tags, Notes and Title blocks. These may be saved either within a Project as an "in-place" Family or as an external .rfa file which may be used in many projects.

Remember Annotation is only seen in the view it is inserted. Thus if you have a Floor Plan, insert Room Tags, and do a duplicate without detailing of the Floor Plan then the Room Tags are only visible in the original view.

Important: Annotation Families will not be seen from another Model if you link this Model into it.

Hosted Families

These are actually a subset of the Loadable Family, however worth mentioning. When installing a window in your new house, you must have a wall to hang it on. A window cannot sit in empty space without a wall, neither may you add a window to your Model unless you have a wall to place the window. These Families are created using a host and must be built to interact with a wall, floor or ceiling.

This is accomplished by choosing the correct template when creating the family. Always choose a host template when starting a family which needs to be hosted by a wall or ceiling.

In-Place Families

Identify any unique or single-use element which your project requires. If your project requires an element which may be useful in more than one project, create it as an independent loadable family otherwise you might consider the In-Place Family.

In-place elements are similar to loadable Component Families however are unique elements which you create only when you need a component which is specific to the current project.
You may create the in-place geometry which references the project geometry; resizing or adjusting accordingly if the referenced geometry changes.

When you create an in-place family, Revit creates a family for the in-place element, which is saved as an integral Component of the Project Model and is only accessible from within the one Project Model.

If this family is to be used extensively in the Model it is usually best to create this as a loadable .rfa family because this saves on system memory in the project and you never know when down the road you might need to use it again on another Project.

Creating an in-place element involves many of the same Family Editor tools as making a loadable family.

We shall spend a little time on basic principles of the family, which are essential to know when creating new content. As most of you realize everything new is built on the foundations and understanding of the old. You cannot create anything new without an understanding of the underlying principles which govern the building blocks of your creations.

For those of you new to Revit and accustomed to AutoCAD, you may think of a Revit Family being similar to the Dynamic AutoCAD Block on Steroids.

It is much easier to make than an AutoCAD block. The important difference in Revit is Families may contain multiple customizable parameters which bring a lot of information and intelligence to the Project Model.

The parameters you create for the Family may be used in your schedules to provide the owner with important information such as size, qty. and data.

These same parameters will govern size, material and misc. information which you might need to schedule embedded in the family.

Revit is a "Parametric Three Dimensional Modeling Software". The operative word here is "Parametric". Most of Refit's flexibility and power comes from the information built into the family.

Parameters are Properties which you assign to the Family when creating one. These are seen in the Properties Palette when a Family is selected.

When creating an "In-Place" Family, the command is found in the ribbon at the Architecture tab | Build panel | Component drop-down | Model In-Place

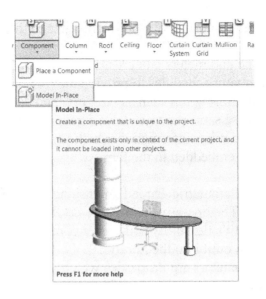

In the Family Category and Parameters dialog, select a category for the element, and click OK.

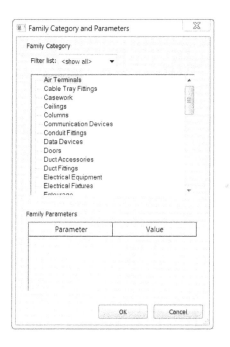

The category chosen will be the category under which the family for the in-place element will be found under "Families" in the Project Browser.

In the Name dialog, give it a name, and click OK.

Name

Name: Air Terminals 1

OK   Cancel

The Family Editor will open. Use the Family Editor tools to create the in-place element.

When you finish creating the in-place element, click the check mark above "Finish Model". In the "In-Place Editor" panel.

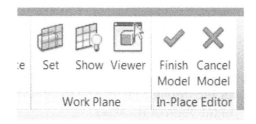

:e   Set   Show Viewer | Finish Cancel
                        | Model   Model

Work Plane | In-Place Editor

An understanding of the Family is basic for Revit to become intuitive.

Families, as we will study them, are similar to miniature stand alone Models, which may be loaded to the main Project Model. The Family is a Model in Miniature and may be a 2 Dimensional Symbol, 3 Dimensional Solid Element, Annotation, and Schedule, View or Title block. All of these types represent variations of possible Families.

Just as you created Blocks in AutoCAD. It is even easier to create your own Families in Revit. The Revit user interface comes with an internal "Family Editor" designed for this purpose. The Family Editor looks and behaves identical to the Revit Interface you have been comfortably using.

The Family Editor

To start building a new Revit Family you need to open the Revit Family Editor. The Editor is a subset of the normal Revit User Interface ribbon which you see when starting Revit.

There are four methods to open this editor:

Method 1 – Open at the Start up Splash Screen by Selecting the New, Open, or New Conceptual Mass, under the Families section of the Splash screen.

Method 2 – Select the large "R" applications menu on the upper left corner of the screen. Select "New".

Because you are creating a new Family you will be asked which Template to start with.

Selecting the correct template can speed the work of building a new family as it creates many of the views, hosts and standard parameters for the type of family you are building.

Note the variations of wall and ceiling hosted family templates. Also note the Annotation and Title Block families are in different directories.
If there is no appropriate selection for your Family use the Generic template.

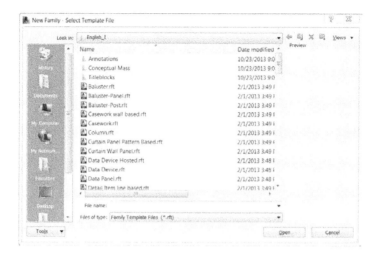

Method 3 – Highlight an existing Family Component Element in the Project's view and then select "Edit Family" from the Modify tab of the Ribbon.

Method 4 – Select a similar Family in your Model which you need to edit and Double click.

Whichever method you use to start the Family editor you get the same results. It opens an Interface similar to the one you have used in Revit, only with a reduced command set limited to the tools you will need to work on your family

Family Editor Interface

Revit Applications Menu

Quick Access Bar   Workflow Tabs   Properties
Panel

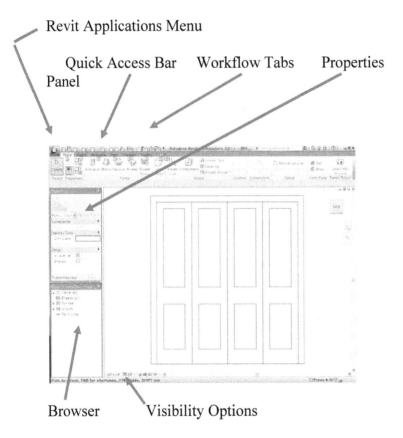

Browser   Visibility Options

The Family Editor will open by default to the "Create" Tab. The "Create" Tab has tools for building 3D forms, inserting other Revit Components, Model lines, Flip Controls, Connectors, Drawing Reference planes, creating multiple Types and loading the Family into your Project Model.

There are several things of interest we need to explore about the Ribbon Interface before we start using the Family Editor.

Selecting the large "R" on the upper left corner of your display will open the same commands as the "File" Pull down. This is the same commands you would see in the Revit Model, such as Save, etc.

To the right of the Tabs, at the top of the ribbon there is a small button. This button will control the level of detail the Ribbon displays. Adjusting this to your satisfaction will make working with Revit easier by gaining screen space. Toggling the button will change the manner the Panels display and will change your screen real estate. Play with this and see how you prefer the Ribbon to be displayed.

Tool Panels (below the TABS) may be dragged off of the Ribbon and parked on the screen. This may be especially handy if you are using Dual Screens or need to often refer to a Panel which you do not want to re-select.

When restoring these panels back to the ribbon, just click on the symbol at the upper right of the panel bar after selecting the panel.

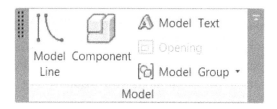

The Quick Access Toolbar at the top left of the screen allows you to locate additional tools which you often access, so they may be easily accessed. Right click on any of the tools in the Tab/Panels and select "Add to Quick Access Toolbar" to add standard commands to the Quick Access Tool.

You rapidly come to realize the context logic about the tabs. When seeking an individual function, think about the logic of where you might find the command. Are you needing to Insert something or create Annotation?

The Create Tab Panels include the Properties selections, 3d Forms, Model lines, inserting other components, Model text (which is different from annotative 2 dimension text), Flip Control, Connectors, Reference lines, and the Work Planes.

The Insert Tab and its associated Panels provides tools for importing and linking CAD files and Raster images into the Family, and also are used when loading nested Families.

The Annotate Tab provides the dimension tools, Symbolic tools, Detail Group, Masking Regions and text.

The "View" Tab and its associated Panels provides tools for controlling line weights, Graphics, and View Creation. Here you will find Visibility Graphics and the "Thin Lines" command under the Graphics panel. The Windows panel has the Switch window, Close Hidden windows, Replicate views, Cascade, and Tile commands.

The User interface permits you to enable or disable navigation and adjust the Browser Organization and Keyboard shortcuts.

When ready to test your Family the Load into Project command is in the Family Editor panel.

The "Manage" Tab and its associated Panels are used for Management commands. Here commands which control the settings of the Family Editor. Things like Project Units, and Shared Parameters.
Materials, Snaps, Units, Transfer Project Standards, Purge and Shared Parameters are located on the Settings panel.
This is also the home for the vital "Load into Project" command.

The "Modify" Tab and its associated Panels provides the commands for modifying and changing your Family objects.

The Properties Panel allows access to the Properties; Type Properties, and assigning the Family to its Category.
The Geometry panel hosts the commands to Cut, Join, Split and Paint.
Naturally the Modify Tab also hosts the Modify panel where you access all of the Modify commands.
The Measure panel has the Aligned Dimension tools.

The Create Panel commands include Groups and Create Similar.

Family Editor Tools

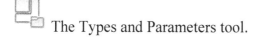

The Types tool **Create tab | Properties panel | Types Property**) will open the Family Types dialog box. Using this you may create new family types (variations in size or materials) or add new instance and type parameters.

The Properties tool opens the Families Properties Palette.

The Types and Parameters tool.

These are the tools you will use to draw 3D objects for your Models. The Solid tool **Create tab | Forms panel**

provides access to tools which create solid geometry using extrusions, sweeps and blends.

The Void tool **Create tab | Forms panel** provides access to the tools which cut solid geometry out of the family. This has its own similar set of 3 dimensional extrusions, sweeps and blends. Creating a void requires more memory resources when a Model opens, so do not over use the Void forms. It can slow your Model.

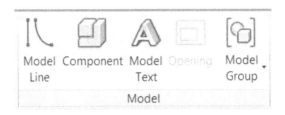

The Model panel contains the tools required to Model objects in your Family. For instance the Model Line tool on the **Create tab | Model panel | Model Line** will draw two-dimensional geometry Model lines. Model lines are visible in 3 Dimensional views. You control their visibility in plan and elevation views by selecting the lines and typing "VG".
The Model Text tool **Create tab | Model panel | Model Text** lets you add signage to a building or letters to a wall. Remember Model Text is visible in 3 dimensions.

The Component tool **Create tab | Model panel | Component** selects the type of Element to be inserted into the Family Editor. After selecting this tool, the "Type Selector" becomes active.

The Detail Component tool **Annotate tab | Detail panel | Detail Component** will place a detail component.

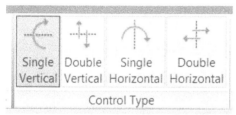 The Control panel has access to choose the Control types which gives you options for the flip arrows you might need in your family."

The Control tool **Create tab | Control panel | Control** will place arrows to rotate and mirror the family's geometry. The following arrow controls are available on the Place Control tab | Control Type panel:

Single Vertical
Double Vertical
Single Horizontal
Double Horizontal

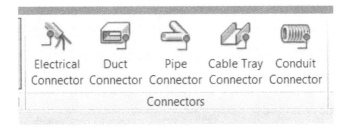

The Connectors panel provides the entry to using MEP connectors in building your Family.

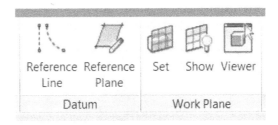

The Datum and Work Plane panels provide important tools for the Model. The Reference Plane tool **Create tab | Datum panel | Reference Plane** creates a reference plane, which is an infinite plane which serves as a guide for drawing lines and geometry.

The Reference Line tool creates a line similar in purpose to a reference plane, but has logical beginning and end points.

This command is used when loading your finished Family to the Project for testing. The Load into Project tool **Create tab | Family Editor Panel | Load into Project** lets you load a family directly into any open project or family. If more than one Project or Family is opened, a dialog box will ask you to select which open file to load the family into.

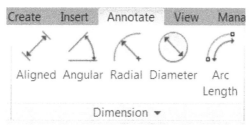

The Dimension panel on the **Annotate tab | Dimension panel** will add permanent dimensions to your family. In creating a dimensional size parameter label it is important to dimension your family before attempting to assign parameters.

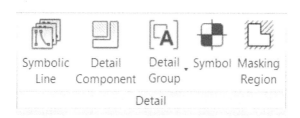

The Detail panel. The Symbolic Line tool on the **Annotate tab | Detail panel |Symbolic Line** will draw lines which are meant for only symbolic purposes. Symbolic lines are not part of the actual geometry of the family. Symbolic lines are visible only in views parallel to the symbolic lines.

The Symbol tool **Annotate tab | Detail panel | Symbol** lets you place 2 dimension annotation drawing symbols.

The Masking Region tool **Annotate tab | Detail panel | Masking Region** will apply a mask which will obscure model elements when the family is used to create an element in a project.

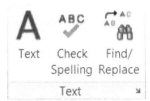

The Text editing panel. Notice this panel has a pull down panel for adjusting and changing the Text properties. The Text tool **Annotate tab | Text panel | Text** will add text notes to the family. This is normally used when creating an annotation family.

2D – Symbolic Lines

A typical Annotation is drawn in 2 Dimensions. Annotation is usually drawn with Symbolic lines will show only in the plane and view where they are drawn. They do not show in 3D views or as an example, if it is drawn in the plan view it will not appear in an elevation views.

Symbolic Lines will show only in the View or axis Plane when the Family is inserted in the host Project. Using Symbolic lines will create Families which are not memory intensive and much more useable in the Model.

A perfect example of this might be of service is the commode. Rather than constructing a 3D object draw the top outline of the top view in the Plan Reference View. When this Family is inserted the Toilet will appear only in the Plan View of the Floor it is inserted on.

Draw a 2D Symbolic rear view on the Back Reference plane. These lines will only show in an Elevation View on the Level your Family is inserted on.

Draw a 2D Profile on the Center Reference Plane of the Family. These lines will only be visible on a Right or Left Elevation of your orientation looking at the Project Model.

The only disadvantage of this type of Family is it will not display if a Section is cut through it.

A 2D Family consumes much less memory than a 3D modeled Family and will lighten the size of your Project Models and your Projects will open faster and perform better. When deciding how to draw a Family, do not overlook the possibility of creating it using 2D symbolic lines. You could be doing yourself and everyone on your team a favor. Always use your judgment when designing a Family.

There is no need to show off your 3D skills to the team. Instead show off your common sense!

The more detailed your Family is drawn and duplicated the greater will be the demands on memory in the Project Model.

If the Family is modeled to the extent which you are showing every nut, bolt and extrusion this will have a very large impact on the ultimate maximum size of your Project Model before it begins slowing down and having poor performance!

Does your door really need to show a detailed lever or knob? Does the corbel actually need all of the detailing you have given it. Over modeling is one of the first things you need to learn to avoid. Because you may, there is a great temptation to show off. Caution your artistic sensitivities with the practical requirements of your project. I recently reviewed a user created Family and could not tell if it was a large dog or a horse. Either way, how important was this to the project for it to be drawn wireframe in 3 Dimensions? A 2 Dimension model would have used less memory and worked well for entourage.

Consider this over abundance of detail multiplied by the number of times the Family might be used in your Project Model. The overall size of the Project file is multiplied by the same exponent. Keeping your Families simple reduces the memory demand placed on the Project Model.

When a Model is opened (unfolded) in the software a Model increases in size by a factor of 20. Thus a 200 Meg model on the server when opened uses 4 gigs of Ram memory.

Many of you may be working on small to medium size projects where this may not be a problem. A large Architectural firm which does major campus projects, Data centers and Hospitals have larger Models and the size and management of large Revit Models is a vital issue which must always be monitored. No matter how much RAM (Random Access Memory) your computer has at its disposal it is never enough.

As you see, it becomes vitally important to consider limiting file size when creating your Families.

Category

Every Family is assigned to a Category in Revit.

Revit uses Categories in much the same manner which AutoCAD uses Layers.

Categories and Sub-categories are important for controlling the Visibility of your Family, and instrumental in determining the AutoCAD layers when exporting the Models Sheet files to CAD.

Whenever creating a Family, it must first be assigned a Category or if no pre-existing category exists build your Family using the "Generic" Category by using the Generic Template.

The major category a Family is assigned to define the default display of the family by controlling the line weight, color, line pattern, and material assignments of the family geometry. To assign different line weights, colors, patterns, and materials to different elements of the family, create subcategories within the major category.

Example: In window families, you could assign the frame, sash, and mullions to one subcategory and the glass to another. Doing this would enable you to assign different materials (wood and glass) to each subcategory.

Family Properties

Family Properties are controlled by parameters and these parameters come in two important flavors.

The Family Type Property exists globally in all Families. When you modify the "Type Parameters" of a Family any changes will globally affect the same parameter of all identical named Families which have been inserted in the Project file. Changes to the Instance Properties effect only the selected Element.

(Do not confuse the "Type Property" with the "Type Family" which will be discussed later).

When planning a Family this distinction becomes important when deciding on the use of the Family. A lot of thinking should happen before you get too far down the road in the building of the Family. How is it to be used? Do you need the flexibility of controlling size or material variations with unique parameters? Should this be a nested family or have multiple Types available?

Instance Properties

A firm understanding of the TYPE and INSTANCE Parameters is essential before you begin constructing your own Families.

You will have to plan which Parameters should be Global and which the Designer should be able to change individually through Instance parameters.

When planning a Family you must decide what types of Parameters will be required, and what adjustable functions, materials and schedule tags will your Family need before commencing the building of the parameters. This requires a little prior planning.

Annotation Families

When creating or editing an Annotation tag it is important to use the Annotation template. Due to the mystical nature of Revit it only displays the tools which you need so to use tools for Annotation Families you must be in a proper Family or Template.

Annotation Families are used with Tags, View Titles, and any type of symbol annotations which the Project might need.

A Label acts as the text placeholder and may be added to tags or Title Blocks. A label is added as part of a tag or Title block family while in the Family Editor. When you place the label in a tag or Title block in the project, you place substitution text for the label, often reading from a project parameter or formula the label will contain project information which will show in the Family.

Start by opening an Annotation Family. For our demonstration we will create a room tag based on the National CAD Standards which will read the Room Finish Parameters assigned by the Room Areas properties.

We will start by drawing the borders of the Tag using 2 Dimension Symbolic Lines.
Symbolic Lines are Drafting Elements and will only appear in the view the Family is inserted as drafting elements. Thus being in the Plan Reference View this tag will only appear in the Plan of the View where it will be inserted.

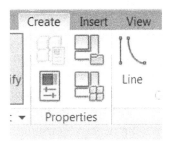

You will notice the Symbolic Lines are now on the Create tab when working with Annotations.

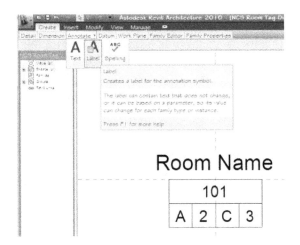

This is 3 /4" wide by 3/8" high. Divided in half and the bottom half divided in fourths.

In the Family Editor select the "Create" tab again and Select the Label command.

If you notice the bottom left of your Revit screen you will notice you are being asked to click to place the Label. On the Alignment panel, select the vertical and horizontal justification. Select the insertion point for the annotation.

Here you select the Parameters to add to this Family.

Add the Room Name, Room Number, Base Finish, Floor Finish, Wall Finish and Ceiling Finish parameters.

Notice to place the Finishes on the same line of the Tag which we modified the Spaces column of the dialog box, we need to change the spaces column to 3. This will offset the insertion location of the labels. We also modified the "Sample Value" of the labels to a single digit format so they will fit in the smaller space allotments.

Note: For this to work in your Project Model, you will have to define a Room area plus add the finish parameters of the Room to display the finishes in the tag.

Annotation Families add content and value to your Project Model. Especially when using Label parameters.

Editing Multi-parameter Labels

You assign single or multiple parameters to labels with the Edit Label dialog.

The Category Parameters window contains the label parameters related to the tag type. The Label Parameters window contains the Category Parameters which display in the label. Typically, this is a single parameter, but you may detail more complex, concatenated labels.

You add and remove parameters by moving them between the windows in the dialog box:

Highlight a parameter in the Category Parameters window and click (Add Parameter) to move it into the

Label Parameters window. Highlight a parameter in the Label Parameters window and click (Remove Parameter) to move it into the Category Parameters window.

Labels display these parameters from the first to the last (top to bottom) as listed in the Label Parameters window. You reorder the label by highlighting a parameter and shift its position using "Move Parameter Up" and "Move Parameter Down".

Shared Label Parameters

Configure the label with the shared external parameters of other families. You configure the shared parameters before moving them over to the Label Parameters window.

Add Parameter. Click this button to enter the Parameter Properties dialog. For Generic Annotation families, you use the Add Parameter button to introduce new Family Parameters to the Generic Annotation family.

Edit Parameter. Click this button to enter the Parameter Properties dialog to edit a selected parameter.

Delete Parameter. Click this button to delete the selected family parameter.

Note when deleting shared parameters they are removed from all sharing labels.

Label Parameter Options

The columns in the Label Parameters window display annotation options applicable for the label. The parameter names are listed in order.

Spaces- Increase or decrease the spacing between parameters by entering a representative number of spaces (zero or greater).

Prefix- You add a prefix to the parameter value by adding a text string in this option.

Sample Value- You change how the default place-holding text appears in the parameter.

Suffix- You add a suffix to the parameter value by adding a text string in this column.

Break- You force a line break immediately after this parameter by checking this box. Otherwise, the text will wrap within the label boundary.

Wrap between parameters only- Force text wrapping in the label to break at the end of parameters by checking this box. If not selected the default is, text wraps at the first word reaching the boundary.

Edit Label Unit Formats

If you create a label with length, area, volume, angle, number, currency, or slope parameter, you format the appearance of the parameter.

In the Edit Label dialog, choose the length or area parameter.
Click and the "Format dialog" displays.

The "Use project settings" option is selected by default. This means the value will display according to the Units setting in the project.

Clear "**Use project settings**"- From the Units menu, select the appropriate unit. From the Rounding menu, select a decimal place value. If you choose Custom from the menu, enter a value in the Rounding increment text box. Select "Suppress 0 feet" to hide leading zeros on dimensions, such as 0' 6". This option is available only for feet and fractional inches.

Graphics Name Description

In the Type Properties of your new annotation Label the following parameters are found:

"**Color**" sets the color of the text or the leader line.

"**Line weight**" sets the thickness of the line which surrounds the text when you select the text and the thickness of the leader line. You may change the definition of the line weight numbers using the Line Weights tool.

"**Background**" sets the background for the text note. With Opaque, the background of the note itself covers the material behind it. Transparent allows you to see material behind the note. This is useful when placing text notes in color-defined rooms.

"**Show Border**" displays a border around the text. Leader/Border Offset Sets the distance between the leader/border and the text.

"**Text Font**" sets the fonts for the text note. The default is Arial.

"**Text Size**" sets the size of the typeface.

"**Tab Size**" sets tab spacing in a text note. When you create a text note, you press Tab anywhere in the text note, and a tab appears at the specified size.

"**Bold**" sets the text typeface to bold.

"**Italic**" sets the text typeface to italic.

"**Underline**" underlines the text.

"**Width Factor**" 1.0 is the default for regular text width. The font width scales proportionately to the Width Factor. Height is not affected.

Applying a Label to a Tag in a Project

In your project, click the Insert tab | Load from Library panel | "Load Family".

If prompted to replace a family of the same name, select "Yes".

In the Project Editor: If you created a window, door, or room tag, and need a host, place one of these components to add your new tag.

If the element does not already have a tag associated with it:

Place the element.
Tag the element.

Click the Create tab | Room and Area panel "Tag", or Annotate tab | Tag panel "Tag by Category".

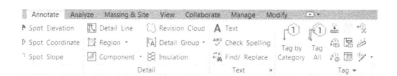

Click the Architect tab | Room and Area panel | Tag drop-down "Room Tag", or Annotate tab | Tag panel "Tag by Category".

Click the Annotate tab | Tag panel | Tag drop-down "By Category".

Select the element which you placed, for example, a door.

On the Properties palette, locate the parameter which you chose when creating the label in either the instance or type properties. Enter a value for the parameter and click OK.
The label value will display in the tag.

Symbol Families

Symbol Families are similar to Annotation Families as these are only two dimensional. You may build any drawing symbol you require.

Many firms do this to make the Revit drawings look similar to the firm's symbolic standards already in their AutoCAD drawings. As a company starts in Revit initially projects are a combination of Revit and AutoCAD. Using similar symbols will avoid a disjointed feel to your printed drawings.

Drawing Symbols are created by using 2D symbolic lines. These lines are similar to Drafting Elements in which they are only visible in the view plane where they were created. If you draw lines in the plan reference view, the lines will only be visible in the plan view where the Family is inserted. If you draw lines, in the Elevation Views of the Family these will appear only in Elevations of your Model.

MEP Families

Revit MEP requires a lot more content than the out of the box software provides.

This content differs from the Architectural products in the families are sensitive to being used by select systems and connection types for ducts, pipes and electrical fixtures creation. These connections must be added to your new MEP Family and identified as the system it is to be used. These must be recognized by Revit MEP to attach Ducts, Conduits and Pipes to your Family.

The Electrical connectors available include Communication, Controls, Fire Alarm, Nurse Calls, Power, Security, and Telephones.

The Duct connectors available include Exhaust, Fittings, Other Air, Return Air, and Supply Air.

The Piping connectors available include Domestic Hot Water, Cold Water, Fire Protection Wet, Fire Protection

Dry, Fire Protection Pre-Action, Fire Protection Other, Fittings, and Sanitary.

Revit MEP 2013 began using "Lookup Tables" when working with components to define the parameter values using an external CSV (command delimited text file) file. This lets you specify multiple part sizes which are based on the lookup table without having to create a separate family type for each size.

This is similar to the Types Catalog which I have already introduced you to. Revit provides the text file lookup function which may be used to transfer the necessary values.

The location of "Lookup Table" files is defined by the **LookupTableLocation** parameter in the new MEP Revit.ini file. Folders may be created for each type of content installed, such as pipe, conduit, etc.

The syntax for the text file lookup function uses the following format: Result=text_file_lookup (LookupTableName, LookupColumn, DefaultIfNotFound, and LookupValue)

"**Result**" is the returned value.
"**LookupTableName**" is the name of the CSV file to lookup.
"**LookupColumn**" is the name of the column from which the result value is to be returned.
"**DefaultIfNotFound**" is the value which will be returned if LookupValue is not found.
"**LookupValue**" is the value to find in the first column of the table.

Part Types

The Part Type parameter provides additional sub classifications of the family categories, and determines the behavior for the parts in the family. The part type serves two functions:

To only allow replacing a particular part with a similar part in a building project.

Type Selector allows you to replace a family of one category with any other family of the same category. However, there are times when this is not appropriate. It would not be valid to replace a cross with a transition. So we have a level of filtering built into the Type Selector for Revit.

The ASHRAE Duct Fitting database is integrated with Revit. This allows calculating losses based on a loss table. To accurately look up the correct fitting in the database, the part type must be defined. If a family category provides a Part Type parameter, the Part Type values available depend on the family category.

Connectors

The difference between Revit MEP components and components for Revit Architecture is the concept of connectors. All MEP components require connectors to behave with intelligence. Components created without connectors cannot participate in system logic.

Connectors are primarily logical entities which allow the software to be used for calculating loads within a project. MEP maintains this information about loads associated with the systems in a project. As devices and equipment are placed in systems, Revit MEP keeps track of the loads based on type of load and system: HVAC, Lighting, Power, and Other.

The loads associated with the spaces may be viewed in the instance properties for each space, and displayed in schedules.

Choosing a Discipline for a Connector

The discipline assigned to a connector determines the types of systems with which it may interact and how it will interact with other components. Obviously if the connector is for the wrong system this component cannot be placed.

When you add connectors to a family, you may specify any of the following:

Duct connectors are associated with ductwork, duct fittings, and other elements which are part of the air handling systems.

Electrical connectors are used for any type of electrical connections, including power, telephone, alarm systems, and others.

Pipe connectors are used for piping, pipe fittings, and other components which are meant for transmitting fluids.

Cable tray connectors are used for cable tray, cable tray fittings, and other components which are meant for wiring.

Conduit connectors are used for conduit, conduit fittings, and other components which are meant for wiring. A conduit connector may be an individual connector or a surface connector. The individual connector is used for connecting only one conduit. The surface connector is used for connecting more than one conduit to a surface.

Selecting the correct discipline is critical to the content working correctly.

After this selection is made, it cannot be changed without deleting the connector and adding it again under the correct discipline than saving the family again.

Connector Orientation

You may place connectors using the following methods:

Place on Face
This option maintains its point at the center. In most cases, this is the best method for placing a connector. Typically the Place on Face option is also easier to use.

Place on Work Plane
This option allows placement of the connector on a selected work plane. You may imitate the Place on Face

option by specifying the plane and using dimensions to constrain the connector.

Connector Orientation

Fittings (pipe and duct fittings) expect the instance origin of the family to be the intersection of the connectors. There is a point on the fitting where all of the connectors will align. Fittings expecting this alignment should be placed at the original intersection of the Center (Front / Back), Center (Left / Right), and Reference Level work planes.

When you place the fitting connectors, the connector must be placed on the face which is on the X-axis. Unexpected behavior will result when the primary connector is not properly placed relative to the other connectors.

Connector rotation is an important part of the connector placement. This is very important for rectangular connectors. The rectangular connector must be oriented so the width is assigned to the face which is on the X and Y axes.

Connector arrows indicate the direction of a duct or pipe flow when it is being created to complete the connection. This does not indicate the flow direction. In most instances, a connector arrow points outward away from the object to which the connector is associated. The duct or pipe when created will pass through the connector. Modify connector arrow directions by selecting the connector and selecting the flip arrows.

Place a Connector on a Face

In the Family Editor, in the Project Browser, double-click Views (all) 3D Views, and spin the model to view the face where you want to place the connector.
The first connector which you place is assigned as the primary connector. This may be changed later.

Click the Create tab | Connectors panel, and click a connector type, such as Duct Connector. Place the cursor over the face which is on the X axis. After the edges highlight, click to place the primary connector. (By default, this is already selected.) The primary connector is now placed.

Place a Connector on a Work Plane

In the Family Editor, open a plan view and a 3D view so you may see where you are placing the connector.

Click Create tab | Connectors panel, and click a connector type (Electrical, Duct, Pipe, Cable Tray, or Conduit).

In the Work Plane dialog, select the Work Plane to place the connector, and click OK.

Select the connector, move it, and specify instance properties as needed.
You may enter parameter values or associate them with parameters for the component.

Orienting a Connector

When connectors are added, you must verify which connector arrows align in the direction from which the other components may be connected, and that the width and height are properly oriented with respect to the component.

In the Family Editor, in the Family Browser, open the 3D view and select the connector to be oriented.
To specify the direction for this connector arrow, select the connector, and click the flip control.
To rotate the component's connectors select the connector. Click Modify | Connector Element tab | Modify panel "Rotate".

Linking Connectors

In the Family Editor, open a view containing the connectors being linked. Select the connector. Click Modify | Connector Element tab | Connector Links panel "Link Connectors". Then select the connector which will be linked to the first connectors.

Unlinking Connectors

In the Family Editor, open a view containing the connector being unlinked. Select the linked connectors. Click Modify | Connector Element tab | Connector Links panel "Remove Link".

Deleting a Connector

Inside the Family Editor, open the view containing the connector being deleted. Select the connector, and press Delete or click Modify | Connector Element tab | Modify panel "Delete".

Connector Labels

Each system connector has a label and leader which displays the system type and connector data, typically the size, flow direction, and flow/fixture units.

Selecting the system device (equipment or fixture) displays the connector labels. A leader line displays from each connector to a system symbol outside of the bounding box of the fixture. Click the system type icon to start the draw command and inherit the existing size and elevation from the connector.

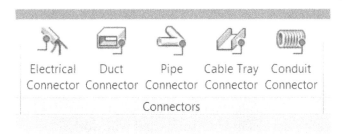

3D Drawing

Which of you who have used Revit may feel like you understand the concept of how to draw in 3D. This may be a false assumption. Currently you may not have been creating true 3D shapes, only using pre-existing 3D families, which others have created in the 3D environments.

We are now going to look into the tools needed for drawing 3D shapes. We will create 3D solids and voids using the following tools:

Solid Extrusion
Solid Blend
Solid Revolve
Solid Sweep
Swept Blend

These same tools are also available for creating Voids or negative spaces in your solids and will work in identical fashions.

We will show how to use each of these tools in the next few pages. Anyone which has taken an Art class is already aware complex shapes are only accumulations of simpler shapes. By creating a multitude of 3D Forms you may build almost any shape.

Revit gives you the ability to draw simple 3D shapes so you may use these to build more complex shapes.

Play with these 3D tools until you become proficient. Before you get carried away with these tools, just remember to stop and think. Just because you can, should you create an 3D family? Building a 3D family is memory intensive on the Project Model. Will Symbolic two dimensional lines serve your purpose better? The more complex the Family, the larger your Model file.

Solid Extrusions

These are the easiest and the most versatile of the shapes and the most commonly used three dimensional shapes.

Creating an Extrusion

A solid or void "extrusion" may be the easiest of the 3D forms to create. You first sketch a 2D profile of the shape on a work plane, and then extrude the profile perpendicular to the plane.
The following procedure demonstrates the method for creating a solid or void extrusion.

To create a Solid or Void extrusion

First determine the Work Plane you wish to create the shape on. Set the Work Plane by clicking the Create Tab | Work Plane Panel | Set.

In the Family Editor, on the Create tab | Forms panel, do any of the following:
Click (Extrusion) or if creating a void Click Void Forms drop-down | (Void Extrusion).
Using the sketching tools draw the extrusion profile on and parallel to the designated Work Plane:

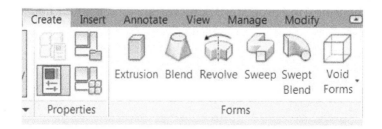

To create a single solid form, sketch a closed loop.

To create more than one form, you may sketch multiple, non-intersecting, closed loops. Remember an individual extrusion must be a closed loop.

On the options Menu set the depth of the Extrusion, in sketch mode, on the Options Bar enter a value for the depth of the extrusion in the "Depth" text box. This changes the location of the end point for the extrusion. To change direction depths may be negative values.

You may also modify the depth of the extrusion on the Properties palette. Specify the values for the start and end points. You may also resize the extrusion in a 3D view by selecting and dragging it.

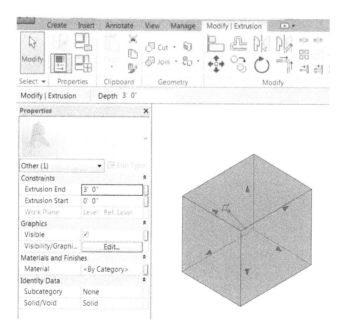

An interesting effect which you may use when defining a Solid is to create a void within the solid you are drawing, by drawing a second closed polygon void extrusion within the border of the first profile a 3 dimension void is created.

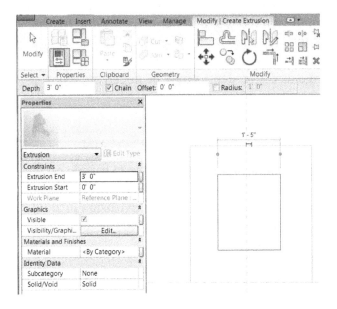

Now look at the 3D view.

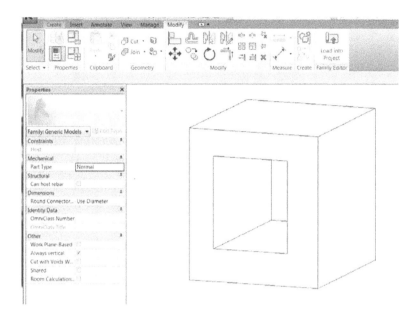

Blends

The Blend tool merges 2 profiles together. For example, if you sketch a large circle and a smaller circle on top of it, as the base and top profile, Revit blends the 2 shapes into one using the proper depth setting.

Always remember when creating a 3D form you may start it anyplace you have created a Work Plane.
In the Family Editor, on the Create tab | Forms panel, you may do any of the following:

Extrusion Blend Revolve Sweep Swept Void
                                   Blend Forms

Forms

Click "Blend", or if creating a void Blend Click Void
Forms under the drop-down | "Void Blend".

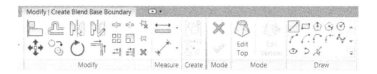

On the Modify | Create Blend Base Boundary tab, start
your base profile using the Draw tools to sketch the
base of the blend, for example sketch a circle.

To specify the depth of the blend, use the Properties
palette, to do either of the following:

To specify a depth which is calculated from a default
start point of 0, under the "Constraints" parameters, for
Second End, enter a value. When specifying the depth
which is referenced from a start point other than the
default of 0, under Constraints, enter the "Second End"
and "First End" values.

When finished with the base profile, on the Modify |
Create Blend Base Boundary tab | Mode panel, select
"Edit Top".

On the Modify | Create Blend Top Boundary tab, use
the drawing tool to sketch a boundary for the top blend,
for example to make this different we will draw a

square.

On the Modify | Create Blend Top Boundary tab, click the Mode panel | and select the green check mark to complete the command
.
Check this in the 3D view. The two shapes have merged transforming from a circle to a square.

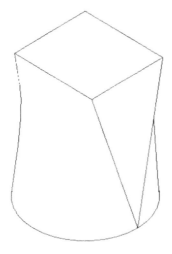

On the Properties palette, look at the blend properties:
To set the visibility of a solid blend, under the Graphics parameters, for Visibility/Graphics Overrides, click Edit, and specify your visibility settings.
To apply a material type to a solid blend family by category, under the Materials and Finishes, click in the Material field, click, and specify the desired material.
To assign the solid blend to a subcategory, under the Identity Data, for Subcategory, select or create a desired subcategory.

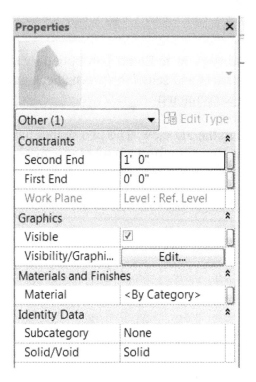

Editing a Blend

In the sketch area, select and highlight the blend. If in the project, click the Modify | Element tab | Mode panel, click "Edit Family".

This moved you to the Family Editor. In the Family Editor, select the blend in the sketch area again.

On the Options Bar, you may change the depth of the blend by entering a value in the Depth text box to change depth of the blend.

On the Modify | Blend tab | Edit Blend panel, select an editing option:
Click "Edit Top" to edit the top of the blend.

Click "Edit Base" to edit the base of the blend.

On the Properties palette, you may change the visibility, material, or subcategory of the blend.

On the Mode panel, click "Finish Edit Mode". Sweeps

Revolves

The secret to drawing round 3D shapes, such as domes or doorknobs or anything which might be turned by a lathe is the Revolve command. This is an important tool in your arsenal.

A revolve is a 3D form which you create by revolving a shape around an axis. You may revolve the shape in a circle or any percentage of a circle.

To create a solid or void revolve in the Family Editor, on the Create tab | Forms panel, do one of the following:
Select "Revolve" or Select Void Forms drop-down | Void Revolve if you need a void.

Create an axis of revolution, on the Modify | Create Revolve tab | Draw panel, click (Axis Line).

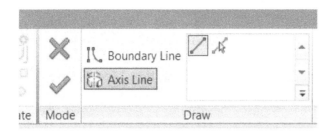

Specify the start and endpoint of the axis.

Switch to "Boundary Line" to create the revolve profile. Use the Draw tools to sketch the profile to revolve around the axis; click Modify | Create Revolve tab | Draw panel | Boundary Line.
On the Properties palette, adjust the properties of the revolve parameter.

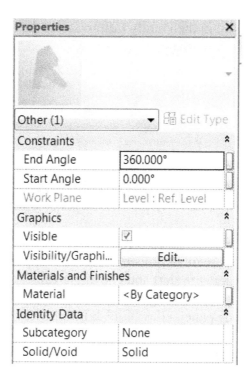

A revolution does not have to be 360 degrees. To change the start and end points of the geometry to revolve, enter a new Start and End Angle.

To view the magic, open a 3D view.

To resize the revolved image in the 3D view, you may select and use the grips to change it.

Editing a Revolve

In the sketch area, select your revolved 3D shape.

If you started in the project environment, on the Modify | <Element> tab | Mode panel, click "Edit Family".

This puts you in the Family Editor, select the revolved shape in the drawing area again.

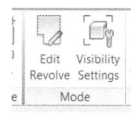

Click Modify | Revolve tab | Mode panel | Edit Revolve.

If desired, modify the revolved sketch.

To edit other revolve properties, on the Properties palette, change the start and end angle values, visibility, material, or subcategory.

On the Mode panel, click "Finish Edit Mode".

Notice you may control the degrees of revolution by adjusting the start and end angles.

Creating a Sweep

The Sweep Tool is used for creating families which require you to sketch or apply a profile (shape) and extrude the profile along a defined path. Sweeps may be used to create anything with a consist profile such as moldings, railings, or simple balusters.

A Sweep is similar to an extrusion except instead of using a depth parameter to define your 3D shape you specify a path for the profile of your shape to follow.

To create a solid or void sweep

In the Family Editor, the Create tab | Forms panel, you may start by selecting "Sweep".

Next you will define the sweep path:
To sketch a new path for the sweep, click Modify |
Sweep tab | Sweep panel | (Sketch Path).

The path may either be a single closed or open path.
Multiple paths are not allowed. The path may be a
combination of straight lines and curves, and it need not
be in the same plane.

To select an existing line for the sweep, click Modify |
Sweep tab | Sweep panel | Pick Path. To select edges of
other solid geometry, such as extrusions or blends, click
Pick 3D Edges on the ribbon. Or pick the existing
sketch lines.

On the Mode panel, click "Finish Edit Mode".

You may Load an existing profile or sketch a new
profile. To load a profile:
Click Modify | Sweep tab | Sweep panel, and select a
profile from the list.
If the profile you need has not already been loaded in
the project, click Modify | Sweep tab | Sweep panel |
Load Profile to load a profile.

On the Options Bar, use the X, Y, Angle, and Flip
options to adjust the position of the profile.
Enter values for X and Y to specify the offset for the
profile.
Enter a value for Angle to specify the angle of the
profile. The angle rotates the profile around the profile
origin. Entering negative values will rotate the profile
in the opposite direction. Click Flip to reverse the
profile.

When the profile is aligned correctly, click Apply.
Select the path, and in a 3D view, zoom in to see the
profile.

To create a new profile:
Click Modify | Sweep tab | Sweep panel, verify <By
Sketch> is displayed, and then click "Edit Profile". If
the "Go to the View" dialog displays, choose the view
where you want to sketch the profile, and click OK.
Generally the profile will be drawn perpendicular to the
sketch path.

The profile sketch may be a single loop or multiple
closed loops which do not intersect. Sketch the profile
near the intersection of the profile plane and the path.

Profiles must always be closed loops.

Click Modify | Sweep | Mode | Finish Edit Mode. Whenever using the sketch command in Revit it must be finished before proceeding with the next step.

On the Properties palette, specify the sweep properties:

On the Mode panel, click "Finish Edit Mode".

Swept Blends

A Swept Blend is the combination of both the Sweep and Blend tools. This creates a 3D shape which follow a designated path yet morphs itself at both ends of the geometry. The shape of a swept blend is determined by the 2D path you either sketch or pick and the 2 profiles you either sketch or load.

To create a solid or void swept blend

In the Family Editor, on the Create tab | Forms panel, select "Swept Blend".

Specify the path for the swept blend. When creating a new path select "Sketch Path".
Click "Sketch Path" to sketch a path for the swept blend.

Click "Pick Path" to pick existing lines and edges for the swept blend.

To select edges of other solid geometry, such as extrusions or blends, select the Pick Path. Or pick existing sketch lines, watching the status bar to know what you are picking. This method locks the sketch lines to the geometry you are picking and permits you to sketch the path in multiple work planes, hence possibly creating a 3D path.

On the Mode panel, click "Finish Edit Mode".

The end point for Profile 1 on the swept blend path is highlighted.

The next step is to load a profile: Click Modify | Swept Blend tab | Swept Blend panel, and select a profile from the Profile drop-down.

If the profile you need is not loaded in the project, click (Load Profile) to load the profile.

Use the X, Y, Angle, and Flip options to adjust the position of the profile. These options permit you to refine the position of the profile in relation to the path. Enter values for X and Y to specify the offset of the profile.
Enter a value for Angle to specify the rotation angle of the profile. This angle rotates the profile around the profile's origin. You may also enter negative values to rotate in the opposite direction. Click Flip to flip the profile.

To create a custom profile you select on the Swept Blend panel, verify "By Sketch" is selected and click the "Edit Profile".

If the "Go to View" dialog displays, select the view where you want to start your sketch of the profile, and click OK.

Use the tools on the Modify | Swept Blend | Edit Profile tab to sketch the profile. Profiles must always be closed loops.

On the Mode panel, click "Finish Edit Mode".

Click Modify | Swept Blend tab | Swept Blend panel | Select Profile 2.

Load or sketch Profile 2 using the steps same steps you followed for profile 1.

You may, edit the vertex connections. By editing vertex connections, you control the amount of twist in the swept blend. You edit vertex connections in plan or 3 dimension views.

On the Modify | Swept Blend tab | Swept Blend panel, click "Edit Vertices".

On the Edit Vertices tab | select "Controls on Base" or "Controls on Top".

In the drawing area, click on the blue grip controls to move the vertex connections.

On the Vertex Connect panel, click the "Twist Right" or the Twist Left tools to put additional twist in the swept blend.

When finished, click Mode panel | "Finish Edit Mode".

To apply a material to a solid swept blend, under Materials and Finishes, click in the Material field, select and specify a material.

To assign a solid swept blend to a subcategory for additional visibility control, under the Identity Data parameters, for Subcategory, select or create the subcategory.

Editing a Swept Blend

In the sketch area, select the "Swept Blend". If you are in the project environment you may change to the Family Editor by selecting on the Modify | Element tab | Mode panel, click "Edit Family".

In the Family Editor, select the swept blend in the drawing area.

On the Modify | Swept Blend tab | Mode panel, click "Edit Swept Blend".

If you need to edit the path, on the Modify | Swept Blend tab | Swept Blend panel, select "Sketch Path".

Use the tools on the Modify | Swept Blend | Sketch Path tab to modify the path, and click Mode panel | Finish Edit Mode.

If you need to change one or both of the profiles, click on the Modify | Swept Blend tab | Swept Blend panel, click "Select Profile 1" or "Select Profile 2".

On the Swept Blend panel, select a different loaded profile from the drop-down list, or select "By Sketch" from the list to sketch a new profile.

If you selected "By Sketch", click "Edit Profile" on the Swept Blend panel.

Sketch the profile and then select the Mode panel | Finish Edit Mode to finish editing the new profile. Select the Mode panel | Finish Edit Mode to finish editing the sweep.

Just as we created Solid 3d Objects Void 3D spaces may also be created.

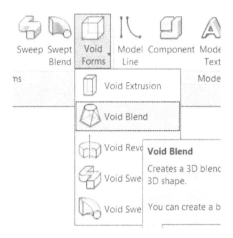

As you may see, all of the Void tools hide under this pull down.

Conceptual Massing

This method of drawing masses works in 3D so you are not dependent on plane views. The Massing Family has automatic work plane detection and permits you to work freely in 3D space. The Conceptual Family supports a dragging tool similar to Inventor. This is called a "Gizmo". The new tool permits intuitive and flexible 3D forms making use of complex lofted surfaces, spline by points, x-ray mode, adding profiles and edges to your geometry. This tool allows more complex and elaborate 3D shapes to be added to your Model.

These mass shapes may be divided by patterns to panelize and further define the shape. Mass Floors and Wall surfaces may be added to your mass using the "By Mass" selection commands. This makes the mass shape a quick way to start the conceptual design of your structure.

The Conceptual Family provides three predefined Reference Planes. You may easily create more as needed. The Revit Conceptual Design Environment (CDE) provides the design tools early in the design process for architects, to quickly create and express ideas in the design which may be integrated into the building .Use this environment to directly manipulate a design's points, edges, and surfaces into forms.
After creating the mass this may be used in the Revit Project Environment as the basis from which you create more detailed architecture by applying walls, roofs, floors, and curtain systems "by face". You may also use the Project Environment to schedule floor areas, and to conduct preliminary analysis and generate early reports. The Conceptual Design Environment is similar to the Family Editor where you create conceptual designs using in-place and loadable mass family elements. Once the mass(s) are finished they may be loaded into the Revit Project Environment.

To enter the conceptual design environment.
.

Conceptual Mass Family

To begin creating Conceptual Masses select "New Conceptual Mass" under "Families" on the Splash Screen. Conceptual Masses is a Revit Family Template style.

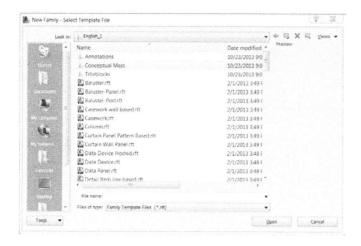

Select the Mass.rvt template to start.

Another Method to start a Conceptual Mass is to Click the Revit Application menu (Large R upper left corner of screen) | New | Conceptual Mass.

In the New Concept Model dialog, select "Mass.rft", and click Open.

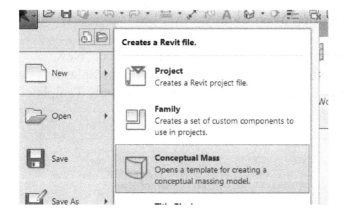

Your initial sketching area will contain three pre-defined Work Planes.
Start by selecting one of these planes and select the appropriate drawing tool.

Once the footprint of your structure is drawn the Ribbon creates a new tab "Modify | Place Lines.

Select Forms | Solid Forms. Your footprint than becomes a three dimensional mass with grips which may be used for editing.

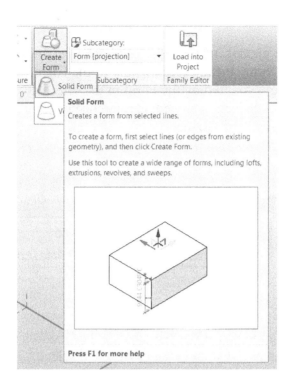

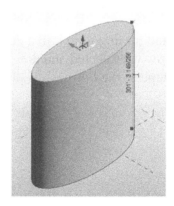

Please note the "Gizmo" grips on the selected top surface of our mass. Selecting grip points or the "Gizmo arrows will permit you to edit changes to the mass by dragging.

The 3D gizmos, may be dragged to change the shape of the 3D form object. Selecting any of the Gismo arrows will allow you to drag the Form in the selected direction. Selecting any edge, reference point or face will activate the Gizmo.

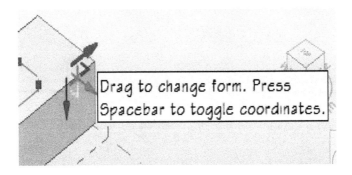

Pressing the Space Bar will change the Gismo's 3D coordinates. By default the Gizmo will select coordinates perpendicular to the face, however clicking the space bar will switch the coordinates back to your World Coordinates.

Select an edge and try dragging it in a new direction. In the example below we selected and dragged two edges to change the shape of the Form.

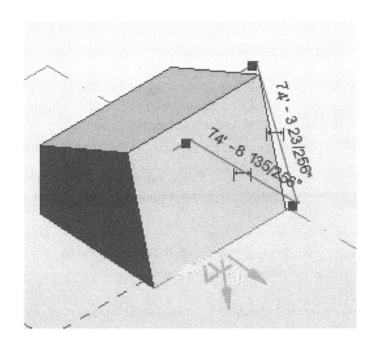

Dissolving Form Elements

You may dissolve a form to its underlying editable profiles.
To dissolve a form, select the form. Click Modify | Form Element tab | Form Element panel | Dissolve.

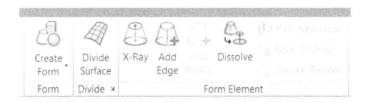

The form drops all surfaces and leaves behind the profile curves and paths. You then edit curves and paths of the profiles as needed or add additional profiles to your mass.

Another tool in Conceptual Massing is the "X-Ray command. This makes the mass translucent and you are able to grab the profiles and perform edits of the profile.

The "Form Element "Panel also contains tools for adding edges, additional profiles, locking and unlocking the profile.

The Divided Surface command will permit you to divide the selected surface by grids and patterns.

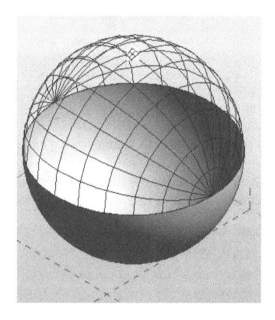

Please note the spacing or number of grid lines is set from the "Options" bar. Complex shapes may also be created using the 3D Spline curve. By using this command irregular and complex solids may be created.

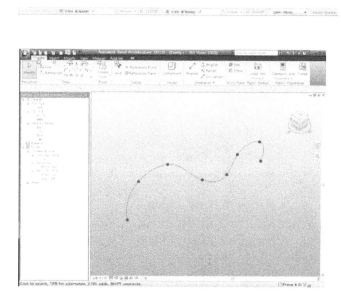

Select the Spline and click on Create Form. After creating the Form we added a Profile to the middle

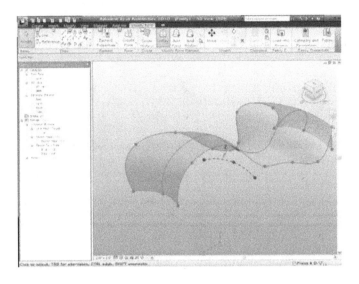

3D Reference Points may be added to your Massing Family. When selecting the Reference points the Gizmo will pop up allowing you to drag and position the Reference Point. There is also a tool, which will create Reference Points on a Spline curve for exotic shapes.

Reference points may be used as constraints on your shapes to define your mass.

The best way to learn this new tool is to get in and experiment with it.

Parameters

Parameters provide the power which gives Families so much versatility. Parameters are assigned when building a Family or may be added to existing Families.

Each time you open a Properties Dialog Box you see a list of available cells to select. These are Parameters. These listings in the Dialog Box may be used to change the size of the Element, affect information such as Model Numbers or Materials for scheduling and any number of other uses. I also use a text parameter in Families which I create to advise people who the author was who created the family, when it was created and the date it was created.

There are two varieties of Parameters.

The first is the "Instance Parameter". These are Parameters which may be edited individually and only affect changes to the single Element (Family) which was inserted in the Model.

The second is the "Type Parameter". These are not changed "on the fly" using the Properties Palette. To edit these you must open the Family Editor, make your change and reload the Family to your Project file. When a "Type Instance" is changed and saved it affects all of this Family in your Projects Model globally.

Do not confuse the "Type Parameter" with the "Type Family". These are two different things and Revit has unfortunately used similar terms, which may cause confusion. As you become proficient the difference in these two will become clear.

A "Type Family" is a Family such as an exterior window, which has multiple sizes such as widths (24", 36", and 48"). Instead of drawing multiple copies of the same Family, one or more Parameters are linked to a parametric dimension, which is changed by creating different "Types" (sizes) in the same Family. If the only difference in your Family is minor for an entire series of objects we may create "Types" listings which will list all of the available differences in the Family when imported in a Model.

When selecting a parameter which has a dependency built from another parameter, all of the related parameters are highlighted in orange.
This provides valuable clues as to how other parameters are dependent and how changes to this parameter will affect other parameters.

New parameters try to auto-classify themselves into the appropriate parameter groups.

When looking at Instance or Type Parameters loaded to your Project. Select the Properties Palette. To view the Type Parameters select "Edit Type" panels.

Below is the Type Property Dialog Box of a Door family. Notice some of the changeable Parameters are the "Height" and "Width".

When desiring to create a Family similar to one already existing "Duplicate" the existing Family and then rename with a unique different name to create a new Family based on the one you copied. In Revit Duplicate has the same meaning as copy.

The Type Parameters in this Family include specific Parameters relating to the size, material or construction details.

The Instance property is a modeless dialog box intended to be always a heads up display on your screen. You access the Type Properties by selecting the element. The Instance Properties display in the Properties Palette.

Now we have finished boring you with covering some of the essential perquisites to understanding and building families, let's get started creating a useful Family and have some fun.

The Family we are going to create for this exercise is a Conference Table. Eventually we will use this same Family to add more of the advanced Parameter Functions.

To get started create a new Family using the Furniture.rft template. Go to the Revit Applications menu select "New" | Family and when the "Select Template File "dialog box comes up select the Furniture.rft. Starting with the correct Template for the type of Family you are creating saves a lot of time and pain because many useful parameters are built into the template.

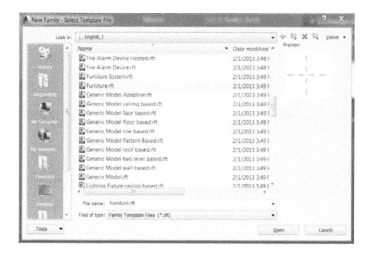

As we explained previously there are two types of lines available when drawing a Family, **Symbolic** and **Model** Lines.

To draw a Symbolic Line in the Family Editor, select the "Annotate" Tab; select "Symbolic Lines" found on the Detail Panel. Symbolic lines are two dimensional.

To draw a Model Line select the "Create" tab select "Model Line" found on the Model Panel. Model lines are used to draw three dimensional shapes and are visible in all views.

Remember Model Lines may be viewed in 3D views as well as other views depending on cutting planes. Symbolic Lines are only seen in the flat View where they are drawn. Sections will not cut Symbolic lines.

Reference Planes and Lines

In the Family Browser let's start by selecting the "Front View" of the Furniture template.

We are going to create some Reference Planes to be used in constraining the Family. These will also be very useful later in drawing the Solid shapes.

A reference plane acts as an invisible 2 dimension floor or wall with infinite extents, running through the family model. Though you only draw a short line it acts as an infinite plane in all directions.

To draw a Reference Plane, in the Family Editor, Select the "Create" tab, and select "Datum Panel" on the Work Plane tab. The Modify | Reference Plane Ribbon will assist you in drawing the reference plane.

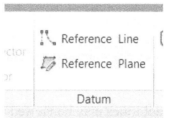

First we create the framework (or skeleton) of your Family. The framework is comprised of reference planes and parameters which you will later use to add the actual geometry. The position of the framework also will define the origin (insertion point) of the family.

Reference planes differ from Work Planes a Reference Line is a perpendicular plane and is a surface you may build on. The crossing point of two reference planes which are designated as **"Defines Origin"** in the Properties Palette will serve as the insertion point of your Family. When using a reference plane it is important to give the plane a name in its Properties Palette, so you may always identify it. Some Families become quite complex and naming the reference planes will assist in identifying the plane.

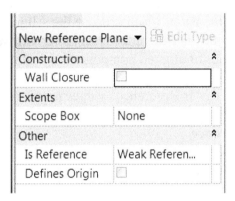

When using a Family template the point of origin (insertion point) is predefined for you. If you wish to change the origin you may define the family origin by selecting two Reference Planes as the definition, then pin (lock) them in place and check the box in Properties "Defines Origin". This becomes the insertion point of the family. Most default family templates create predefined origins, but you may need to re-set the origin for some families if you desire a different insertion point.

Check the "Defines Origin" box in Properties if setting a Reference Plane as a new origin. Notice a Reference Plane may also be set to a "Strong Reference" or a "Weak Reference" in the "Is Reference" parameter. The difference between a strong and weak reference is whether dimensions in the Project Model will snap to it. This means you may dimension to the family or align to it. If you set a reference plane as a reference for all family types, then you may consistently dimension to the family type.

The "Is Reference" parameter found under the "Other" parameters in the Properties Palette also sets a reference point for dimensions when you use the Align tool. Specifying the "Is Reference" parameter will select different lines of aligned components for dimensioning.

The following "Is Reference" values may be set:

Not a reference
Strong reference
Weak reference
Left/Center (Left/Right)
Right
Front
Center (Front/Back)
Back
Bottom
Center (Elevation)
Top

To dimension families placed in a project, you need to define the family geometry Reference Planes as either "strong" or "weak" in the Family Editor by modifying the "Is Reference " parameter in the planes properties..

A strong reference has the highest priority for dimensioning and snapping. Temporary dimensions snap to any strong references in the family. When you select the family in the project, temporary dimensions appear at the strong references. When placing a permanent dimension, the "strong" references in the geometry will highlight first. A weak reference will be the lowest priority for dimensioning. When attempting to place a dimension, you may need to press "Tab" to select a weak reference, as any strong references will highlight first.

Finish constructing the remaining framework by drawing the remaining reference planes. After placing the reference planes as shown in the sketches below, we will define the framework parameters.

Set a Reference Plane defining the height of the Table in the Front View. Sketch this plane anywhere then position it by modifying the temp dimension. Draw a second reference plane 3" below the "Table Top". Escape from the Reference Plane command, click on the plane you just created, right click, than select "Properties". Name this Reference Plane "Table Top". Naming a reference plane is important to keep track in complicated families. Name the lower reference plane "Table bottom". When the reference plane is selected the name of the reference plane displays in the viewing area.

Consistency and accuracy is important when naming items in Revit.

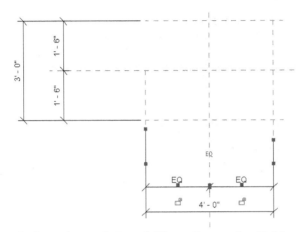

Switch to the Ref. Level Plan, Create the Table perimeter boundary reference planes. In the Ref. Level Plan View draw four more reference planes each centered from the intersection planes as shown. The initial sizes of the table will be 3'-0" x 4'-0". Dimension these using the Annotation aligned dimension tool.

Note: by right clicking on the continuous 2'-0" dimensions and selecting the "EQ" which appears near the string these dimensions will be constrained to each other and maintain the same relationship to the insertion point. As we change the size of the table it will remain symmetric around the insertion point axis. Make the end dimensions of 1'6" equal also.

This completes the borders and height references for our Conference Table Family.

Please note the insertion point of your future family will be the intersection of the two dashed reference planes which were pre-existing when you started your

Family Template. If you are curious you might examine their properties and look at the "Is Reference "settings.

Parameters define and are linked to the Reference Planes. At this stage these Parameters usually control the size (length, width, height) of the Family. The Family's lines or solids are snapped and pinned to the reference plane thus when the Parameters values are changed the Reference Planes move in relation to these changes and the appearance of the Family Model follows the changes in the Reference Planes. Drawing a line over a reference plane now automatically creates a relationship of the line to the plane. In the older versions of Revit all lines had to be pinned (locked) to the location plane.

If in our family you want to be able to dimension to the edges of the table, you must set the "Is Reference" property of these reference planes to "Strong" in the Type properties of the reference planes. When you dimension to this table in the Project Model you will then be able to select either the origin (insertion point) or the table's edges or both to locate and dimension the Table in the Project Model.

Dimension Parameters
We will now use the dimensions assigned to the reference planes to create an adjustable "Length" and "Width" Dimension Parameter. Select the Length Dimension. Right click and select "Label". Then select "Add Parameter" as shown in the figure below:

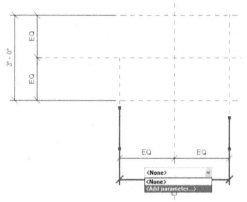

The Parameter Properties dialog box will appear:

In the Name field type in "Length" as shown. Under the "Group Parameter" select "Dimension" from the pull down.
Select the "Instance" radio button. This is where you choose to make your Parameter an Instance or a Type.

In this exercise we want the parameter to be an Instance type. (If you do not understand the difference between Instance and Type these are crucial concepts and now might be a good time to review.")

Click "OK". You will notice the dimension of the overall length of the table has changed to a parameter variable named "Length".

Repeat these steps to set the Table Width dimension and the Table height dimension as Parameters. Then, create Labels for these also.

Next we will set the Work Plane by going to the "Create tab | Work Plane | Set".

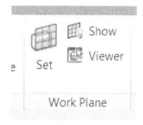

The following Dialog box will appear. Set the Work Plane to "Table Top". This is where we will create our first Solid. By setting our work plane to this level all of our dimension sizes will be in reference to this level when creating the table top.

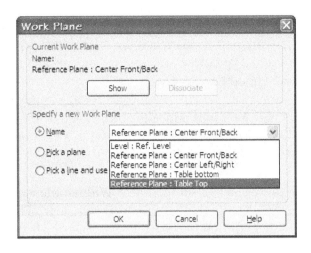

We will begin by drawing an extruded Solid for the Table Top. As you will remember we set the Work Plane to "Table Top" so the extrusion will be drawn at the top level, thus when entering the depth of the extrusion we will use -3" so the bottom of the Table top will be drawn with a thickness originating below the top of the work plane. This will give us a table top 3" thick. (Review Solid Extrusions if you need to.)

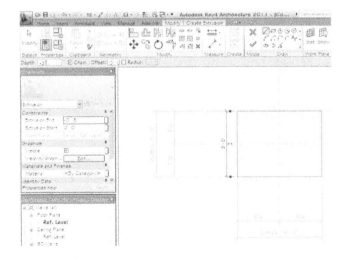

Notice in the "options bar" the depth has been set to -3"
and we have sketched a closed loop for the extrusion.
Finish the extrusion by selecting the green checkmark
on the Mode panel of theribbon.

After creating the Solid Table Top we now address the
Table legs.

You will note in the figure below we will add
Reference Planes for the legs, constrained to 4" wide
and also constrained to 6" from the Table perimeter.
These will be used to draw and constrain the
relationship of the legs to the table surface.

In a Family when you place a dimension it will act as a
constraint. The dimension does not show in the views
when inserting a family; however the dimensions will
constrain how the family geometry behaves. When
placing a dimension as a constraint you need to lock
them, by selecting and clicking the lock icon.

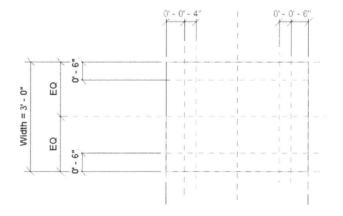

In the figure below we will use the Solid Extrusion
Form command to draw both legs. Sketch the edges of
the extrusion to align with the intersection of the
reference planes.

In an elevation view. Drag your leg to the appropriate
extrusion using the arrow grips and lock these
extrusions to the bottom of the table and to the
Reference Level 0'0" by selecting the lock icon and
closing the locks.

In the Plan view lock the outside edge of the legs to the
inner reference planes.

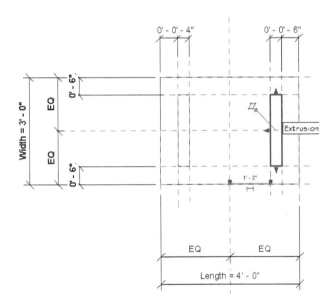

Switch to the three dimensional view and examine your
table by rotating it through the axis. Does it look like
the figure below? If not you may have missed locking

the leg to a needed reference plane. Always test your Family after each step!

To Flex the Family you must insert the Table Family in a Revit Project. Here you can select the Family and adjust the dimensional constraints that were set previously.

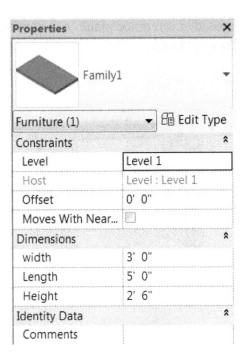

The next step will be to Flex the model and insure the dimension parameters, which we created, will control the Length, and Width and Height of our model.

Change the Length to 6'-0" and click OK. The Table should change in length to 6'. After adjusting the size of your table, open it in 3D view and rotate the Table through its axis verifying the performance of your parameters. Make sure the table legs move with the change in length. If they don't you have something amiss.

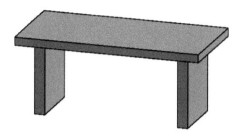

If the Model is not performing as expected, check all of the extrusions are locked to their associated Reference Planes or recreate the Dimension Parameters constraints to fix the problem.

Nested Families

More complex families may be created by using copies of existing families nested into your family. We have created a nicely functioning table; however what good is a table without chairs? Let's add some comfortable chairs to the family.

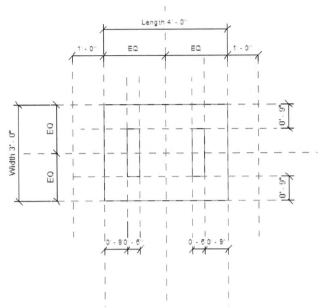

Add Reference Planes 1'-0" from the ends of the table.

These will be used to control the distance of the chairs from the table for consistency as the table size changes.

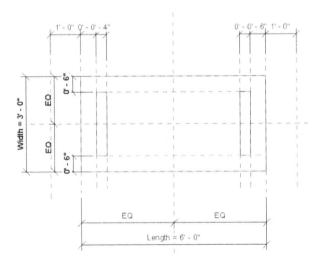

On the Create tab | Model panel select "Component". This will ask if you need to load a Family. Go to the Furiture directory of the Imperial Library and select the "Chair-Task Arms.rfa" family. Insert this into your Table family. (Hint pressing the space bar before inserting will rotate this chair in 45 degree increments).

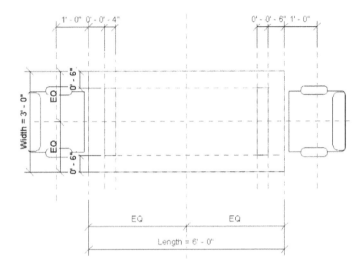

Note the new Family now shows in the Project Browser under the Families organization.

Be sure to constrain these chairs to the Table edge. We have added a nested Family. The advantage in doing this is to save time instead of drawing individual chairs.

Next step is to change the Length of the Table in the Family Types Property box and check to make sure the chairs will move with the table.

To place additional chairs in your Family select Component under the "Create | Model" tab and you may now select this chair from the Type Selector found on the properties panel.

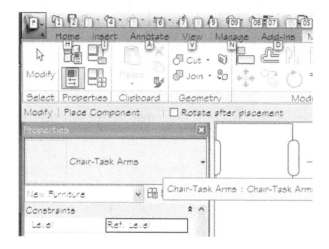

Take a look at your new creations in three dimensions and flex your family through several changes in the table length.

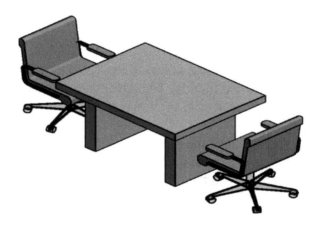

There are restrictions regarding the type of families which may be loaded and nested in other families:

1. Annotation families may be loaded only into other annotation families.
2. Only detail families and generic annotations may be loaded into detail families.
3. Model families, details, generic annotations, section heads, level heads, and grid heads may be loaded into model families.

Multiple Family Types

Instead of creating a lot of Families for different size elements you may be pleased to know you may create one Family and assign it a multiple number of sizes using the parameters we created. Thus the same table style may be one family which may be inserted using a multiple number of sizes.

Additional sizes are added in "Family Types". To open the Family Types dialog box go to the Create tab | Properties panel and select the "Edit Type" icon.

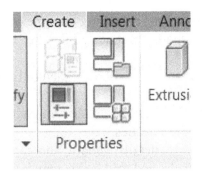

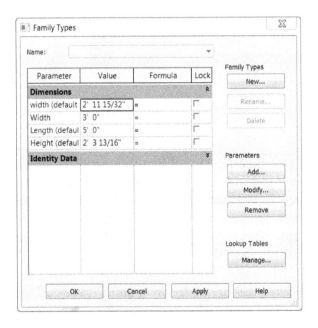

The Family Types dialog box will appear. To change and save a new value to an existing parameter select "New", and give it a name. In this example I am making a five-foot long table.

The width or height of this table may be easily changed by adjusting the Length and Width parameters. Place the new value for the Length of the table and click on "Apply".

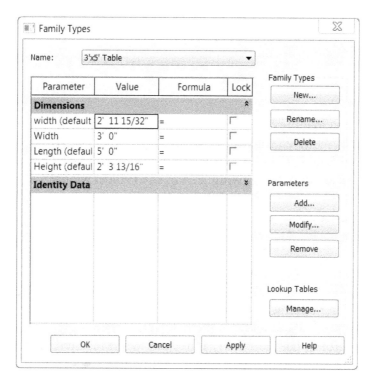

Notice in the pull down list of Types at the top of the dialog box we have created a new type. 3' x 5' Table. Using the same procedure we create several other sizes like 3' X 6' and 3' x 8' and 4' x 12'

By selecting any of these Types in this pull down list and selecting "Apply" you may change the size of the table. The size parameters are saved with the Type.

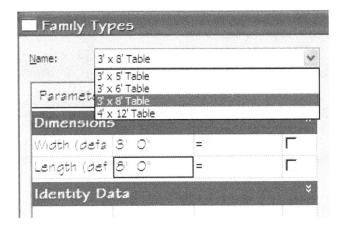

When loading this Family to a Project, each of these sizes will load into the Projects "Type Selector". Any length table may be selected in the Project to be inserted into the drawing area of the Project Model.

One family loaded with many sizes ultimately saves time sweat and work.

Material Definitions

When building a new Family you may need to assign a Materials Parameters to the Family. This not only controls what the Family looks like when inserted in the Model, but also effects how it will render.

Because different tables might be made from different materials we will assign a Material Parameter to the table top as an Instance Parameter. You may remember by assigning this as an Instance Parameter each inserted instance of the Table in our model may have its appearance adjusted individually instead of globally.

Return to the Family Editor.

Open the Family Types dialog under Create tab | Properties Panel and select the Family Types Property.

Click the Add button in the Parameters grouping.

For the Name, type "Tabletop Material".

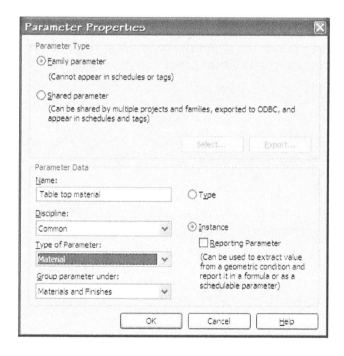

Select Material in the "Type of Parameter" box.

Choose "Material and Finishes" under the Group Parameter.

Choosing the "Type of Parameter" will influence the type of data the field in the Properties will contain and how the Parameter will react.

Parameters may be selected from the following types:

Text - is a customizable type. This may hold any type of text data.

Integer - The value in this field is always expressed as an integer. A formula may be substituted in the numeric field.

Number - Is used to establish the length of an element or subcomponent. A formula may be substituted for the number.

Length - Is used to create a Length parameter of an element. This may be used in formula to calculate area. Formulas may be substituted in this field.

Area - Is used to establish the square footage of an element. Formulas such as (Length Height x) may be used to calculate this field.

Volume - Is used to establish the volume of an element. Formulas may **also** be used in this field to calculate volume.

Angle - Is used to establish the angle of an element. Formulas may also be used to calculate this field.

Slope - Is used to create parameters which define slope.

Currency - May be used to create currency parameters.

URL - Provides web links to a user defined URL.

Material - Establishes parameters for a specific material to be assigned.

Yes/No – This is a Boolean response and is used for instance properties when the parameter is defined with either a Yes or a No.

Family Type – Used with nested components and will allow you to swap Family categories.

The difference between a Family Parameter and a Shared Parameter is Family Parameters will not appear in Schedules. A Shared Parameter may be scheduled and will appear in tags when shared by multiple projects and families.

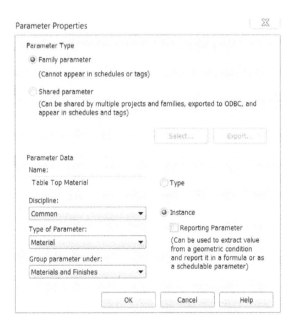

Click "OK" to create the parameter and then "OK" again to exit the Family Types dialog.

The parameter is now available to use in the Family.

Select the tabletop extrusion, right click and select the Properties.

Note we now have a Materials and Finishes in the Properties dialog box.

Next step in assigning the Materials parameter is to load this Family into a Project. Because we are assigning an "instance" property it may only be set inside a Project.

Beneath the Materials and Finishes grouping, select the browse button.

Choose the Tabletop Material parameter and then click the browse button.

We have chosen Instance here so we may have the option to assign different material finishes to each individual instance of the table we insert into a project Model.

The Materials Dialog box should appear. We will now assign some defaults for this particular material.

In the search box type the material you are looking for. Such as Wood. The available materials will show in the Search Result box.

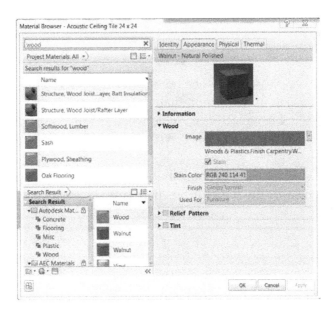

Next on the "Render Appearance Tab".
Scroll down and choose the appearance of the Table
Top to be used when rendering. In this example we
have choose a Walnut top. Minor adjustments to this
may be made by selections in the Appearance tab.

Next select the "Identity" tab of the Materials Browser
dialog box. Here you may enter specific manufacturer's
information.

The Table Top should now take on its own default appearance when looked at in the 3D view of the Project when Realistic is selected on the View Options Toolbar.

Family Parametric Arrays

As our Table changes in length (or even width) we are going to desire to seat more people at the table. Instead of creating multiple copies of this Family, we may adjust the number of chairs and the seating pattern by using the Parametric Array properties of this Family. Thus as the Table increases in size the Family will automatically display (and schedule) the correct number of chairs.

Along the length of the table, we want to vary the quantity of chairs as the length of the table changes.

To accomplish this, we will use an array with a custom parameter.

Create a Ref Plane offset 12" out from each of the other edges of the table. Create two more reference planes 1'3" from the center of the table.

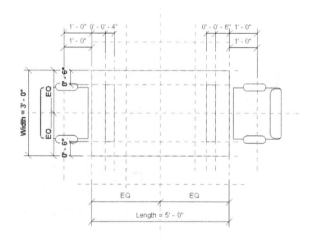

Next select the same chair we previously added at the ends of the table. Place it vertically to make it sit just under the edge of the table on the centerline reference plane. Next
Mirror it along the axis of the table to create a copy above the table.

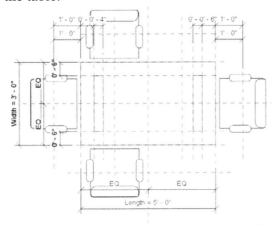

Select both chairs (the original and the mirrored copy) and click the Array icon.

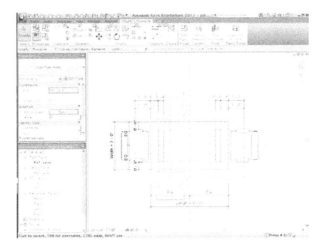

Make sure the "Linear" Array and "Group and Associate" options are selected on the Options Bar, set the Number to 2 and choose the "Move to Last" option.

When the Group and Associate features, are selected the array remains parametric by grouping the selected entities and retaining the array parameters for later editing. This enables you to select any arrayed item later and vary the quantities or spacing to adjust the entire array.

For the start point of the array, click the chair and then move to the right horizontally and click again nearby.

Array the chair horizontally along the length of the table. We may edit the quantity of arrayed items later, but you may experiment with different values now to see how it works. Remember to return the count to 2 before continuing. When building an array in a family, it is critical to build it in a few steps as we have done here. This allows you to check you are assigning the proper settings and parameters as you proceed.

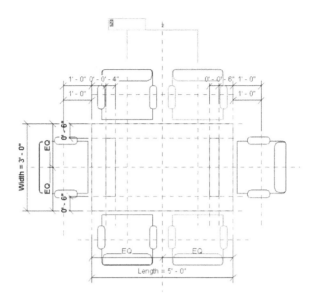

Using the Align tool, align and constrain (lock) the center of the chair to the Ref Plane we added above and then repeat on the other side. Lock the chairs at the end of the table to the other reference plane. Click the Modify tool to finish the task. When using Align, always highlight the reference edge first: in this instance the Ref Plane, and then the center of the chair.

Clicking either chair the array dimension will appear showing a current quantity of 2.

Flex the model and apply the 8-foot Type. Try the 6-foot Type next. The chairs should now change quantity.

When you flex the smaller table Types, all the chairs end up on top of one another. We may solve this by associating a new parameter with the array dimension.

Reapply the 8-foot Type and then click "OK".

Click any chair and then click directly on the array dimension. Select the "Create | Types" Property under the Parameters section select the "Add Parameter" function.

For the Name type "Chair Count". We will leave this Parameter Group setting to "Other". The Parameter Group assigns a header for this parameter in the Properties dialog box. Click "OK". This will be the quantity of chairs along one side of the table.

The next step is to assign numerical values for the number of chairs required for each size of the table family.

Open the Family Types dialog. The Chair Count now appears as a new parameter under "Other".
For the 6-foot Type, set the count to two and then "Apply".
For the 8-foot Type, set the count to three and then "Apply".
For the 12-foot Type, set the count to five and then "Apply".
Flex your model to test each Type and then click "OK". This is an effective way to vary the quantity of chairs in a logical manner, rather than creating each Family individually.

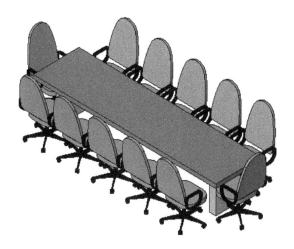

When we test this Family in a project, you will note each chair counts individually under the quantity cell of the schedule.

Profiles

Profiles are flat two-dimensional shapes used to produce the more complex three-dimensional geometry. Profiles are used in Families to create Solid Sweeps for complex three-dimensional shapes.

Think of a Profile as a cross-section of a complex Solid. When creating Sweeps instead of drawing the intricacies of a section you have the option of using a prebuilt or custom Profile.

The use of profiles provides many advantages:

1. These are simple Families drawn outside the project and may be saved as RFA files which may be used in any project.

2. Like other Families, a profile family may contain flexible parameters and locked constraints. This permits more power and control over the profile shape than a simple sketched shape.

3. Similar to Families, a profile family may contain multiple Types.

4. Profile Families behave perform well with other nested Families. Since they are self-contained, they do not behave in unexpected ways when the parent Family flexes.

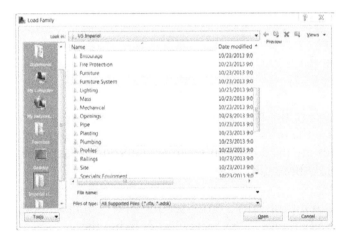

Revit comes with prebuilt profile Family templates such as: Mullion, Rail, Reveal and Stair Nosing.

Revit also provides a generic "Hosted" template and finally a simple Profile.rft template to serve if something more custom is required.

Use the mullion template in "Curtain Walls" if creating a custom curtain wall mullion shape. These mullion profiles may be loaded to the Project and assigned to your default curtain wall design in Element Properties.

When working in the Family Editor, there are two solid forms which may use a nested profile Family rather than a sketched shape. These are Sweeps and the Swept Blend.

To use a profile in a Family you are creating, first create the new Profile Family based on the appropriate Profile.rft template. Draw the shape adding any parameters, constraints or types. Save this Family and then load it into the Family you are creating. Once the profile is loaded, you may use it in creating the solid forms.

Flip Controls

You have noticed some Revit Families include flip controls which allow you to flip and mirror the family instance with a single click.

These controls may be added to any Family.

Let's look at how Flip Controls are added to a Family. Start by opening the Family you wish to add the Flip Control too and select the Ref. Level floor plan view.

On the Create Tab, select the "Control" panel.

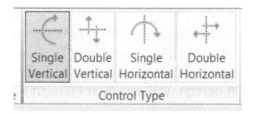

Select the double vertical arrow icon on the Options Bar and then place the control above the plan graphics by clicking it in place.

You may now Save the file and load it into a project to test the new Control.

Families above the cut Plane

A problem may occur in a Family when all of the geometry is located above the cut plane of the view. This will affect the visibility of the Family in a plan view if it is designed to be outside the normal view range.

Light switches and overhead ceiling mounted elements or wall-mounted components may fall outside the View Range.

If all you want is for the Family to appear in reflected ceiling plans, then this is no issue.

If you wish to have an element's geometry completely above the cut plane, and appear in plan views, you must employ extra steps.

Begin by adding an element in a Family file which does intersect the cut plane. If you have a sconce or other wall mounted feature and you want it to appear in dashed lines on the plan to indicate it occurs above the cut plane. Normally, it will not appear in plan because Revit must find geometry when it cuts the plan view, otherwise nothing is shown.

If there is no geometry of the family intersecting the cut plane, Revit will not display this item. In an elevation view within the Family file, add a vertical Symbolic Line passing from the Family and down through the cut plane. Draw it using an "Invisible Lines" type. This ensures the line will not be visible in elevation views, but will give Revit something to cut which will trigger the plan display. This will create dashed Symbolic Lines in the plan view to represent the overhead object.

Importing Manufacture's Content

Sometimes it would be nice to import content from a manufacturer's site and not have to re-create your own. Increasingly manufacturers are providing Revit Family content.

Because building a Family requires time therefore money many people are still not generous with sharing content they have created with possible competitors.

Sketchup files may also be imported into Revit; however these will not contain parameters and will be shape only.

Workflow for Building a Family

1. Before beginning family creation, take some time and **plan the family**. What category should it be created in and which parameters will your family need?

2. Create the new family file (.rfa) starting with the appropriate startup family template. How will the family be hosted in the model? This will get you started in the correct Category for the Family and this will save a lot of setup time. Each template comes with the appropriate hosting, reference planes, category and preexisting parameters which will allow the faster creation of the Family. Is there a similar existing family you may borrow from?

3. Define and create any subcategories needed for the family to help control different visibilities of the geometry.

4. Create the family skeleton, or framework using Reference Planes. These reference planes may be controlled by parameters.

5. The insertion (origin) point of the family is the intersection of the major reference planes.

6. Assign Labels to flexible dimensions which will be used for Parameters. You will need to qualify whether these will be Type or Instance labels. Will the size change globally for all aspects of the family (Type) or for the uniquely selected family (Instance)?

7. Test and flex the reference plane framework. It's best to do this before getting too far down the path. Flex after any new parameters are created. This is often the

first stage where families will go pear shaped. Labeled dimensions in the family may be stretched and pulled in 3D views, with the mouse to flex and test the relationship of the Family.

8. Add the visible geometry by creating the solids, voids or lines over the reference planes.

9. Flex the new Family again to verify the correct component behavior. Does anything seem malformed or twisted? Fix any problems now.

10. Specify the 2D and 3D geometry display characteristics with subcategory and entity visibility settings. Is there anything you would like to hide or be displayed as a different color or material? This is where you may put subcategories in play.

11. Save the newly defined family, and then load it into an empty project for testing. Some family items will not function within the Family Editor and must be tested live in a Project. Did it load properly and does it display correctly? Are the correct Parameters in the Properties Palette?

12. For large Type families which includes many parameters, such as varying sizes or varying materials create a Type Catalog to save the multiple possible variations of size/materials of the Family.

Suggestions for Naming the Family

Families should be named in a manner providing the users with as much information as possible. This should be a standard agreed to by all of your team members and published.

One possible method might be to name them by

Category-Subcategory-Description-Type Size

Certifying (checking) the Family

The content specialists should be a review point in which any Family should be checked before being adopted as a company standard.

Some of the things which easily slips by the creator and should be reviewed are:

Is the Family Name correct and easily understood in relation to your naming standards?

Was the Family created in the correct Category?

Does the Family flex correctly in all views (plan, section, elevations, and in 3D?

If the Family was built with dimension parameters, do they work?

Does the Family schedule correctly?

Often times a second set of eyes reviewing your families is very useful before incorporating to your company as a standard.

Autodesk Seek

Autodesk Seek is a web service which allows designers, architects, engineers and students to search for and find manufacturer or generic products. When you have created new families which may pass the Autoseek requirements you may publish your Families to Autoseek and share these with others.

Troubleshooting Families
(When families go bad)

Most Family problems may be directed to these problems, Constraint Errors, Load Problems and Display Problems

Display problems may be caused because of many deficiencies. To begin analyzing the problems first look at where the difficulty is occurring.

If it occurs in family Editor: Most common problem may be constraints.

If it occurs in Project after loading the most common problem may be visibility graphics.

If it does not look as expected after flexing; the most common problem is not enough constraints.

This discovery will help to isolate the problem and provide a clue as to where to start looking.

Start by simplifying problems by working backwards and step through the family backwards by undoing each step of the family until the problem is resolved.

Always create a duplicate copy for troubleshooting. You may use the original for reference and if you do find the problem during deconstruction, you may go back to the original and fix without having to rebuild the deconstruction.

Things to check for during the deconstruction:

Check to make sure the family category is correct
Remove all constraints and dimensions
Remove parameters
Replace formulas with values
Check all reference lines
Rebuild and check all parameters
Rebuild Constraints and check the skeleton geometry
Flex using very small values and very large.